Day Trading

A Winning Day Trading Guide and Insights for Beginners

DARRELL FROST

© Copyright 2018 by Darrell Frost - All rights reserved.

The following Book is reproduced below with the goal of providing information that is as accurate and as reliable as possible. Regardless, purchasing this eBook can be seen as consent to the fact that both the publisher and the author of this book are in no way experts on the topics discussed within, and that any recommendations or suggestions made herein are for entertainment purposes only. Professionals should be consulted as needed before undertaking any of the action endorsed herein.

This declaration is deemed fair and valid by both the American Bar Association and the Committee of Publishers Association and is legally binding throughout the United States.

Furthermore, the transmission, duplication or reproduction of any of the following work, including precise information, will be considered an illegal act, irrespective whether it is done electronically or in print. The legality extends to creating a secondary or tertiary copy of the work or a recorded copy and is only allowed with express written consent of the Publisher. All additional rights are reserved.

The information in the following pages is broadly considered to be a truthful and accurate account of facts, and as such any inattention, use or misuse of the information in question by the reader will render any resulting actions solely under their purview. There are no scenarios in which the publisher or the original author of this work can be in any fashion deemed liable for any hardship or damages that may befall them after undertaking information described herein.

Additionally, the information found on the following pages is intended for informational purposes only and should thus be considered, universal. As befitting its nature, the information presented is without assurance regarding its continued validity or interim quality. Trademarks that mentioned are done without written consent and can in no way be considered an endorsement from the trademark holder

Table of Contents

Introduction 5

Chapter 1: How Day Trading Works? 7
   Day Trading Vs. Swing Trading...7
   Buy Vs. Sell 9
   Retail Vs. Institutional Traders 13

Chapter 2: Trading Psychology and Risk Management..17
   Risk Management In Three Steps......................................18
   Why Do Most Traders Fail? 21

Chapter 3: Day Trading Tools and Platforms................24
   What Broker to Use?..24
   Trading Platform and Market Data 26

Chapter 4: Day Trading Tactics 28
   ABCD Pattern..31
      Summary of the ABCD Pattern..................................34
   Bull Flag Momentum..36
      Summary of the Bull Flag Momentum strategy 37
   Top and Bottom Reversal Trading................................38
      Summary of The Bottom Reversal Strategy 40
      Summary of The Top Reversal Strategy 41
   Moving Average Trend Trading....................................42

Summary of The Moving Average Trend Strategy 44
VWAP Trading **45**
Summary of the VWAP Trading Strategy 46
Support or Resistance Trading **47**
Summary of the Support or Resistance Trading 49
Develop Your Strategy **50**

Chapter 5: Successful Trading Guide and Money Management 54
Final Rule **56**

Conclusion 65

Introduction

In this book, I will explain the fundamentals of day trading and how day trading is different from other styles of trading and investing. In the process, I will also describe important trading strategies that many traders use each day. This book is deliberately short so readers will finish reading it and not get bored halfway through and put it to one side.

If you are a beginner trader, this book will equip you with an understanding of where to start, how to start, what to expect from day trading, and how you can develop your strategy. Simply reading this book will not make you a profitable trader. Profits in trading do not come from reading one or two books, but, as I will explain later, profits can come with practice, the right tools and software, and proper ongoing education.

Intermediate traders may benefit from this book's overview of some of the classic strategies that the majority of retail traders use effectively.

The most important lesson that you can learn from reading this book is that you will not get rich quickly by day trading. Day trading is not similar to gambling or playing the lottery. This is the most important misconception that people have about day trading, and I hope you will come to the same realization after reading this book. In fact, statistically speaking, 90% of people who start day trading fail and lose their money.

Chapter 1: How Day Trading Works?

In this chapter, I will review many of the basics of day trading and hopefully answer your questions about what day trading is and how it works. TAs with any art form, tools are of no value unless you know how to use them. This book will be your guide to learning how to use these tools.

Day Trading Vs. Swing Trading

As a day trader, what do you need to look for?
Here are the things you need to know. Basically, you need to look at actions which move relatively predictably. Second, you will change them in a day. You will not keep a post overnight. If you buy shares of Apple Inc. (Ticker: AAPL) today, for example, you will not hold your position overnight and sell it tomorrow. If you hold an action during the night, it is no longer a day trading; It's called swing trading

Moreover, swing trading is a type of negotiation in which the trader hold stocks for a certain time typically on a less than a month duration. It's a completely different trading style, and you should not use the strategies and tools you use for daily trading to participate in the swing trading.

Swing Trading is a very different type of business. The differences between swing trading and day trading are similar to the differences in the ownership of a restaurant and a catering service. Both are about food, but they are very different: they work with different time frames, regulations, market segments and income models. Do not confuse daily negotiation with other types of negotiation just because negotiation involves actions. Before the market closes, day traders don't forget to close their positions.

Many traders do both daily operations and swings. We are aware that we have two different businesses, and we have gone through separate education programs for both types of commerce. One of the main differences between trading day and swing is the stock selection approach. Generally, swing traders search for stocks in firm companies to ensure that their value won't go low overnight. On the other hand, when it comes to daily trading, you can simply negotiate even with those hanging companies. You are not worried about the closing markets. In fact, many of the companies you trade are too risky to keep overnight because they can lose much of their value in this short period of time.

Buy Vs. Sell

Day traders buy stocks in the hope that their price will go higher. This is called buying long, or selling long. When you hear me or a fellow trader saying, "I am long 100 shares AAPL," it means that we have bought 100 shares of Apple Inc. and would like to sell them higher for a profit Going long is good when the market is going higher.

But what if prices are dropping? In that case, you can sell short and still make a profit. Day traders can borrow shares from their broker and sell them, hoping that the price will go lower and that they can then buy those shares back at a lower price and make a profit.

Sharing shares at a low price is also called short selling. When the price has gone lower, you can buy them cheaper than you bought them earlier and made a profit. Imagine that you borrow 100 shares of Apple from your broker and sell them at $100 per share. Apple's price then drops to $90, so you buy back those 100 shares at $90 and return them to your broker. You have made $10/share or $1,000. What if the price of Apple goes up to $110? In that case, you still have to buy 100 shares to return to your broker because you owe them shares and not money. Therefore, you have to buy 100 shares at $110 to return 100 shares to your broker. In that case, you will have lost $1,000.

Short sellers earn profits when the price of the stock they have borrowed and sold falls. Short sales are important because stock prices generally fall much faster than the increase. Fear is a stronger feeling than greed. Therefore, short sellers, if they act correctly, can make incredible profits, while other traders panic and start selling. But, like everything in the market, which has great potential, short sales also carry risks.

When you buy the shares of a company for $ 5, the worst scenario is that the company goes bankrupt and you lose your $ 5. Your loss is limited. But if you sell this company for $ 5 and then the price starts to rise more and more instead of going down, then there will be no limit to your loss. The price can be up to $ 10, $ 20 or $ 100, and yet your loss is unlimited. Your broker wants to return these shares. Not only can you lose all the money in your account, but your broker can sue you for more money if you do not have enough funds to cover your short positions.

If the price goes down, you can ask correctly, why does your broker allow you to sell short instead of selling shares yourself before the price goes down? The answer is that the broker wants to maintain his position in the long term. Short sales offer the investors who own the shares (with long positions) the opportunity to generate additional income by lending their shares to the short ones.

Long-term investors are not afraid of short-term fluctuations.

They have invested in the company for a reason, and have no interest in selling their shares in a short time. Therefore, they prefer to lend their shares to traders who wish to benefit from short-term fluctuations in the market. In exchange for the loan of their shares, they charge interest. Therefore, you must pay interest to your broker for short sales as the cost of providing these shares. If you sell short on the same day, you generally do not have to pay interest. Swing traders that sell short usually have to pay daily interest on their short stock.

Short selling is a dangerous practice in daily business. Some traders are predisposed for a long time. They only buy shares with the hope of selling them higher. I do not have any prejudice. I'll sell if I think the configuration is ready and I'll buy whenever it suits my strategy.

Retail Vs. Institutional Traders

Retailers can be part-time traders or full-time traders, but we do not work for a company and do not manage other people's money. Retailers are a small percentage of the volume in the market. On the other hand, there are mutual funds, hedge funds, and Wall Street investment banks. Most of these trades are based on high frequency trading and sophisticated computer algorithms. On rare occasions, a person participates in the daily trade of these large accounts. By any means, institutional traders have considerable money behind them, and they can be very aggressive.

You can rightly ask: "How can a distributor, like you and I, get to the game later, compete against institutional traders and win?"

Most of the institutional traders' weakness is that they need to take action while the institutional traders can trade freely or stay out of the market as they see fit. Banks need to be active in the market and exchange large amounts of shares at almost any price. A retailer can freely expect the best opportunities.

Unfortunately, most retailers counter this fantastic advantage when negotiating. If you want to overpower the top traders, you need to be patient and take away the greediness in your mentality. It is not about how much your account has but you need to develop discipline, a balance decision, and proper money handling.

Revolutionary warfare is an irregular approach to war in which a group of fighters, such as paramilitary personnel or armed civilians, use military attacks such as ambushes, raids, sabotage and small wars to create a greater military force. The United States Army is considered one of the most dangerous forces in the world. However, they suffered significantly from the jungle war tactics used against them in North Vietnam. The above examples include European resistance movements that fight against Nazi Germany during World War II.

In the revolutionary trade, you are patiently waiting for the chance to enter the financial market to acquire immediate profits while maintaining your risk on a low level. It does not want to defeat or outwit the investment banks. You are simply waiting for an opportunity to reach your daily benefit goal.

Another advantage of being a retail trader is not losing money even on the instability of the market. If the markets are flat, you will not earn money; Only high frequency sellers earn money in these circumstances. Therefore, you should find actions that move up or down quickly in a relatively predictable manner. Institutional traders, on the other hand, trade at a very high frequency and will benefit from "very small price movements," as they are sometimes called, of "a choppy price action."

It is extremely important to stay away from actions that are highly negotiated by institutional traders.

Institutional traders create high negotiations that you need to avoid. As a single retail day trader, you must stick to the retail business area. They do not trade stocks that other retailers do not sell or do not see. The strength of commercial retail strategies is that other retailers also use them. The more traders use these strategies, the better they will work. The more people recognize the line in the arena; the more people buy at that point. This, of course, means that the inventory will increase faster. The more buyers, the faster it will move. That is why many traders like to share their daily business strategies. Not only does it help other traders to be more profitable, but it also increases the number of traders that use these strategies. There is no benefit in hiding or keeping these methods secret.

Chapter 2: Trading Psychology and Risk Management

Here are the three things that make day trading work: (a) trading psychology, (b) critical business methods, and (c) effective and efficient risk management strategy. It is a typical mistake for a beginner to focus exclusively on business indicators and strategies.

A good business strategy leads to positive expectations. It generates more profits than losses over a period of time. But remember, even the most careful strategy does not guarantee success in every operation. No strategy can assure you that you will never have a loss or even go through a series of exchange losses. For this reason, risk control should be an integral part of any commercial strategy.

The trader's inability to handle the money losses is the primary reason for their failure on daily trading operations. It is a common tendency for people to accept profits quickly and also wait until the levels of loss are balanced again. By the time some new traders learn to manage their risk, their accounts are bad, if not irreparably, damaged.

To be a successful trader, you must learn the rules of risk management and then implement them firmly. Learning the risk management strategy and firmly implementing it are the keys to succeed in trading. You need to set boundaries that will limit you to placing decisions. From time to time it will be necessary to admit losing and say: "I was wrong" or "The configuration is not over yet" or "I'm getting out of the way."

Risk Management In Three Steps

Step 1: Before you begin, identify first the maximum money you will place on trading. The money you are willing to risk should not be more than 2% of your bank account.

Step 2: From your entry, compute your maximum risk per share and strategy-stop loss in your chosen currency.

Step 3: To know the total number of shares you can exchange from time to time, divide it with the amount you get on step 1 on the amount you will get on step 2. For instance, having an account of $50,000 will limit you to a transaction of $1000 according to the 2% rule. However, if you want your risk to be smaller, you can choose the 1% rule which will limit you to the amount of $500 per transaction.

Now let's say you view the Apple Stock (ticker: AAPL) for the ABCD Pattern Strategy which I will talk about in Chapter 4. They buy the shares at $20 and want to sell them at $23, with a difference of $18.50. You will risk only $2 per share. This is another way to control your risk.

To determine the size of your stock, you will divide $500 (your transaction limit) by $2 (which is your risk per share) which will get you an answer of 250. This means than you have 250 shares (the maximum shares you can buy and exchange).

On Chapter 4, the different day trading tactics will be discussed. From there, you will understand how stop loss is used based on technical analysis. Your trading plan will also depend on the size of your account which only you will be able to determine that.

The decisions will come from you definitely. For instance, if your stop is higher than your moving average, you need to compute if your stop is higher than your maximum account size at risk or not. If your stop in the moving average result in a $700 loss and has set your maximum loss of $500 per transaction, you need to temporarily pause from trading and patiently wait for another chance to trade.

You can argue that it will be difficult to calculate the stock size or stop the loss based on a maximum loss in your account while waiting to enter operation. You have to make a decision quickly. Otherwise, you will lose the opportunity. I understand that it is difficult to calculate the loss limit and the maximum loss of the size of your account in live operation.

Why Do Most Traders Fail?

Day trading is not supposed to be easy. Trading needs practice, and I strongly recommend that new traders paper trade under supervision for at least three months in a live simulated account. It sounds crazy at the beginning, but you will quickly learn how to manage your account and your risk per trade. You will be amazed at how rapidly the human brain can do calculations on what share size to take and where to set the stop loss.

Day trading requires self-discipline and ability to make immediate decisions. If you hear the latest news that an activist investor has just joined Amazon.com Inc., your first reaction might be to load the boot. I can hear the logic that forces you. "Let's buy 5,000 shares on Amazon! Let's make a big order!" But you need to be able to make a quick decision about whether to buy, sell or sell that inventory, and you need to make that call with discipline.

Your ability to maintain self-discipline and mental control will eventually lead your trading strategies to improve overtime. It's hard enough to know what the market will do, but if you do not know what you're going to do, the game is lost. The new commercial strategies, the tips you will get from me or this book or even the most sophisticated software I can imagine will not help the traders who cannot handle themselves.

Evaluate yourself with the following questions:
- Does this strategy suitable to my trading approach?
- If this my trading strategy won't work well, where will be my stop?
- How much money should I risk on trading that will grant me a chance of winning?

This is what many traders find difficult. All of these decisions, the process that guarantees that these decisions are adjusted to their risk tolerance and strategy parameters, are misleading multitasking. Not only is it multitasking, but also multitasking under stress.

Sometimes, it's okay to push yourself at the edge of your comfort zone when it comes to trading. However, if you feel that you have pushed yourself too far or your trade goes the wrong way, you need to slow down and know where should be your stop.

Chapter 3: Day Trading Tools and Platforms

Like starting any other business and profession, to start day trading, you require a few important tools. You need a broker and an order execution platform. These are tools you will need for yourself.

What Broker to Use?

Please remember that brokers will give you 3 to 6 times leverage. If you put in $30,000, you're going to have $120,000 in buying power (leverage of 4:1 in this case). That leverage is called the "margin," and you're allowed to trade on margin, but you need to be responsible about it. It is easy to buy on margin, but it is also very easy to lose on margin. If you lose on margin, your broker takes the loss from your main money account. Therefore, the margin is a double-edged sword. It provides you an opportunity to buy more, but it also exposes you to more risk. There is nothing wrong with buying in the margin, but you do have to be responsible.

The margin is like a mortgage for your house. You borrow a significant amount of money and buy a residence. Banks will give you a mortgage, but they won't take any responsibility or risk for it. For example, imagine that you put $100,000 down and borrowed $900,000 on a mortgage (10:1 leverage) from your bank to buy a $1,000,000 house. If the price of your house goes up to $1,200,000, you still owe the bank the original $900,000 plus their interest. So the extra $200,000 is your profit that came from margin leverage. You couldn't have bought that house without a mortgage leveraging. Now imagine that the price of the house drops to $900,000. You still owe the bank $900,000 plus their interest, so the drop has hit your main $100,000, and you have lost all of your original down payment of $100,000. That is the other side of leveraging. Therefore, you need to be responsible about when and how much you use your account margin.

When a broker sees that you are using leverage and losing money, they might issue a "margin call" to you. A margin call is a serious warning and day traders must avoid getting them. It means that your loss is now equal to the original money you had in your account. You must add more money, or else your broker will freeze your account. If you need to know more about margin, leverage or margin calls, check the broker's website and do some research on the Internet.

Trading Platform and Market Data

Fast trading is the key to the day trader's success. You must be able to move in and out of trades quickly. "If the broker does not use any software or platform with hotkeys, do not get in and out of trades immediately. With the spikes in stocks, you want to put money in your pocket and make a profit quickly. You definitely don't want to mishandle your orders. They require a quick execution, so I recommend a good runner and a fast execution platform.

DASTrader is a trading platform that is highly recommended to beginners. This type of platform offers various solutions for individual traders, online brokers, commercial shopping centers, enterprises, and distributors worldwide that require smarter execution services.

On a daily basis, I have found their support team very attentive and competent. The DAS servers are connected to the NASDAQ data centers. They cannot be closer to the market to negotiate. DAS trader is not a broker, but you can link your trading account with your platform to ensure the execution of the fast order. Some brokers offer the DAS platform when an account is opened, but IB has a platform that I cannot recommend.

Chapter 4: Day Trading Tactics

"In this chapter, you will be presented with the most used methods that rely on two main components: (1) price level and (2) methodical indicators. It is important to learn and practice these two elements at the same time.

Although some strategies require only technical indicators (such as Moving Average and VWAP), it's helpful also to have an understanding of price action and chart patterns to become a successful day trader. This understanding, especially regarding price action, comes only with practice.

Day traders do not worry about what companies do and how much they profit. As a day trader, your focus should only be on the price level, methodical indicators, and summary of the tactics.

When your stock increased by up to 80%, you will determine what facilitates the growth. "So, it's a biopharmaceutical stock, and they just got FDA approval." or "They just passed through clinical trials. Okay, there's a catalyst, now I can understand what's going on." Beyond that, you won't find listening in on conference calls or sifting through the earnings papers to be helpful. You don't care about those aspects because you are not a long-term investor – you're a day trader. We trade very quickly - guerrilla trading! – at times we trade in time periods as short as ten to thirty seconds.

The volume in the high frequency algorithmic trading reaches for up to 60% when observed on the current market. That means you are trading against computers. If you've ever played chess against a computer, you know that you're eventually going to lose. You might get lucky once or twice, but play sufficient times, and you are guaranteed to be the loser.

The same rule applies to algorithmic trading. You're trading stocks against computer systems. On the one hand, that represents a problem. It means that the majority of changes in stocks that you are seeing are simply the result of computers moving shares around. On the other hand, it also means that there are small stocks traded each day on such heavy retail volume (as opposed to institutional algorithmic trading) that you will overpower the algorithmic trading and you and I, the retail traders, will control that stock.

Each day, you need to focus on trading those particular stocks. These are Alpha Predators, stocks that are typically gapping up or down on earnings. You must look for the stocks that have significant retail traders' interest and significant retail volume. These will be the stocks you will buy, and together, we the people, the retail traders, will overpower the computers, just like in a storyline for the next Terminator sequel.

And please, remember, the philosophy of trading is that you must master only a few solid configurations to be consistently profitable. In fact, having a simple trading method consisting of a few minimal setups will work to reduce confusion and stress and allow you to concentrate more on the psychological aspect of trading, which is what separates the winners from the losers.

ABCD Pattern

The ABCD pattern is the simplest and easiest to follow trading pattern. It is also the best day trading tactic for beginners and intermediates. Even if it has been used for a long period of time, the effectiveness of this strategy still remains since many traders are still utilizing it. The ABCD pattern is widely used, so it is suggested that you use it as well.

The ABCD patterns begin with a strong upward movement. Buyers aggressively buy an action from point A and continue making new highs of the day (point B). You want to enter the trade, but you should not participate in the trade since at point B, you are far away and already at a high price. Also, you cannot tell where your grip should be. You should never enter an exchange without knowing your stop.

At point B, those traders who bought shares previously can start to sell them to gain profit at a low price gradually.

On the other hand, you need to be careful about entering the trade since you are not aware where the fund is coming from. Now, if you find that the price of a stock does not go down on a specific level in point C, it means that the stock can be a potential for profit. Thus, careful planning and knowing when to set your stops and profit taking are essential before trading. Let's take a look at Ocean Power Technologies Inc. (ticker: OPTT) at July 22, 2016, when they announced that they had a new $50 million contract to build a new ship.

The stock surged up from $7.70 (point A) to $9.40 (point B) at around 9:40 a.m. You, along with other traders who had not heard the news, waited for point B and received a confirmation that the stock wasn't going to go lower than a certain price (point C). When you saw that point C was holding as support and buyers wouldn't let the stock price go any lower than $8.10 (C), you bought 1,000 shares of OPTT close C, and your stop was below point C. You knew that when the price went higher, closer to B, buyers would jump on massively. The ABCD Pattern is a very classic strategy, and many retail traders look for it. You purchased stock between points B and C. Close to point D, the volume suddenly spiked, which meant that traders had jumped into the trade.

Your exit would be when the stock made a new low, which was a sign of weakness. As you see, OPTT had a nice run up to around $12.

Summary of the ABCD Pattern

1. If you are watching with your scanner that a stock is surging up from point A and gets a different maximum for the day (point B), observe if the price makes a support higher than point A. If that's the case, don't enter the trade quickly.

2. Observe the stock during its consolidation period. You select your stock size and modify your stop and exit strategy.

3. Enter the trade close the price of point C if it advances to point D or above.

4. Your stop is point C's loss. You need to sell your shares if the price is lower than point C. To minimize the loss, it is important to purchase a stock close point C. To attest the effectiveness of ABCD pattern, some traders patiently wait and buy at point D. However, this type of strategy

puts you more at risk and reduces the chance of getting more rewards.

5. When the price goes up, you can sell half of what you have at point D and take your highest stop to your starting point.

6. If you feel that price is unstable or the sellers are controlling the price level, you can already sell your remaining position.

Bull Flag Momentum

In day trading, Bull Flag is a quick execution tactic that normally works well in short reserve stocks. Bull Flag is a trading strategy that attempts to make many profits. However, this type of strategy does not last long. Once you get the aim, you will immediately take out your winnings and move out.

Bull Flag Momentum is essentially an ABCD pattern that is more likely to occur in low-float populations. It's fast, and it will fade faster. Therefore, it is more or less an impulse growth strategy. Traders purchase when the action is moving. Scalpers seldom buy on a waiting phase.

These types of actions tend to be quick and brutal, so it is important that you only jump if there is confirmation of an outbreak. If you expect the actions to halt the top of the waiting phase area, you reduce the risk and the exposure time. Instead of buying and waiting, which increases the exposure time, resellers wait for the outbreak and then send their order. Come in, get out of the scalp and get out fast. That is the philosophy of impulse drivers:

- Enter the outbreak
- Take your profit
- Get out of the way

Summary of the Bull Flag Momentum strategy

1. If you see a rising supply, wait patiently for the consolidation period. They do not change immediately (you will remember that this is the dangerous act of "hunting").
2. You are monitoring the stock during the consolidation period. You select your stock size and modify your stop and exit strategy.
3. Enter the trading when the price increases above the level of waiting for phase candles. The break below the waiting area phase is your stop loss.

4. Sell half of your position to win the upward path. From the equilibrium point, take your stop loss from the short point of waiting phase.
5. If you feel that price is unstable or the sellers are controlling the price level, you can already sell your remaining position.

Top and Bottom Reversal Trading

Top and bottom reversals are the simplest trading strategies of all. Day traders like to use these because of precise entry and exit points and a high ratio of profit and loss.

These are the four important components of the top and bottom reversal trading

1. There are around five candles that move up or down.
2. The Bollinger Bands, where the stock is traded indicates the volatility aspect of the stocks.
3. RSI analyzes the strength and weakness of a stock. The population that has 90 relative strength index

indicator is overbought. A reversal is to be made when it reaches the extreme level.

You must realize that almost all major movements will eventually be corrected. What goes up must go down again. In reverse strategies, one of the key benefits is the ability to monitor stocks, while calculating possible points of resistance and areas that could offer a good investment opportunity. This allows you to resist being impulsive and trading. Instead, you can take the time to observe the change and wait for the momentum to change.

An important metaphor that many traders use when they talk about reversal strategies is that of an elastic band. When stocks go down, they inevitably have to be corrected. Therefore, when a population is full, you will know that you are going to bounce someday and you want to be there for the bounce. What you do not want to be is the one that is still selling. It's like "catching a knife that falls." When stocks fall, a confirmation about the reversal will be followed up.

Summary of The Bottom Reversal Strategy

1. Observe on your scanner if it shows more than four serial candles that fluctuate. When you see that an action hits your scanner, check its resistance level and volume immediately to determine if its operational or not.
2. While waiting for the reversal confirmation to follow up, you can form a bearish dandelion candle, check that candles that are close or far from the Bollinger Bands and ensure that the relative strength index should not be greater than 10.
3. Buy the action when it reaches no more than 5 minutes.
4. The minimum set of the day determines your stop loss.

5. Your objective to gain profit is to acquire a balance resistance level; the volume weighted average price, a stock that reaches more than 5 minutes which means buyers can take the control again.

Summary of The Top Reversal Strategy

1. Observe on your scanner if it shows more than four serial candles that fluctuate. When you see that an action hits your scanner, check its resistance level and volume immediately to determine if its operational or not.
2. While waiting for the reversal confirmation to follow up, you can form a bearish dandelion candle, check that candles that are close or far from the Bollinger Bands and ensure that the relative strength index should no less than 90.
3. Sell the stock if the action reaches at least 5 minutes.
4. Your stop is the height of the previous candle or the maximum set of the day.

5. Your objective to gain profit is to acquire a balance resistance level; the volume weighted average price, a stock that reaches no more than 5 minutes which means buyers can take the control again.

Moving Average Trend Trading

Some traders use moving averages as possible points of entry and exit for the trading day. Many stocks start a bullish or bearish trend, taking their moving averages in 1 minute and 5 minute charts as a kind of mobile support or resistance. Traders can benefit from this behavior and track the trend along the moving average (next to the moving average for long or lower than the moving average for short sales).

Why do moving averages become support or resistance? The answer is that many traders look at these lines and make decisions based on them. Therefore, they have a self-fulfilling prophecy effect. Aside from that, there is no specific reason to defy why moving averages turn to be a support or resistance.

Summary of The Moving Average Trend Strategy

1. When observing a stock and observe a trend that takes into account the moving average, consider trend trading. They quickly review the trading data on the stock reaction in a minute or 5-minute of the chart the last few days to know its moving average.
2. Once you determined that moving average is most appropriate for commercial behavior, you can buy stocks as support after confirming moving averages and buy closely to the moving average line to acquire a lower price. Normally, your stop is below five dollars upon breaking the moving average limits.
3. You follow the path of moving average until it stops.
4. Continue to monitor the trend and avoid using final stops in this type of strategy.
5. A stock that moves too far from the moving average will get some benefit, usually halfway.

Waiting is not an option for the exit in moving average trend strategy.

VWAP Trading

VWAP is a type of moving average trend strategy that relies on the number of traded shares to the account. Other moving averages are calculated only based on the price of the shares in the chart, but VWAP also takes into account the number of shares listed at any price. VWAP is probably integrated into your trading platform, and you can use it without changing the default value. VWAP is a good indicator of who controls the price action: buyers or sellers. Here, the buyers have full price control. If the price of action falls under the VWAP, it can be assumed that the full price control is gained by the sellers.

Operating with VWAP is simple to use by beginners since many traders studying the VWAP based their decisions on it. Hence, it is easy for a beginner trader to make a right operation on his trading style. However, a stock that attempts to break the VWAP can be lost as it assumes that the trader observing knows he is losing it. As said, the VWAP trading strategy is easy to understand and simple to follow.

Summary of the VWAP Trading Strategy

1. By creating a watch list on VWAP, you have the full control of the price movement. Making a right move in VWAP will confirm later if you have done a resistance or a violation.
2. To minimize the risk, buy closely as possible. Under VWAP, your stop will pause and automatically will close in a 5-minute frame.
3. Continue operating until you reach your profit objective and reach a new resistance level.
4. This type of trading strategy targets to sell the mid position close the profit of support or resistance level. Then, it moves its full stop to the entry point or break-even point.

Support or Resistance Trading

Horizontal trade or resistance trade is the preferred negotiation style. The market knows no diagonals. It is reminiscent of the price level – the logic reason of horizontal support or resistance levels. However, the diagonal trend lines are deceiving and open to subjectivity – a reason to not use it as it can lead to bias, fraud, and illusions. Diagonal trend lines are the most unreliable implements. It traces false lines that can affect prices, movement, slope, and implication. For example, having an attempt to buy can make you draw a trend line a little more abruptly.

Support is a level of price where the purchase is solid enough to reverse a bearish trend. When a bearish trend finds resistance, it runs like a top marathon that reaches the finish line and then continuously moving away from it. The resistance level is denoted by a horizontal line in a diagram that connects more than two lines.

Resistance is a level of price where the sale is tough enough to reverse an up-trend. An uptrend that acquires support is like a person who accidentally bumped by a moving car when he crosses the street then eventually stopped and collapsed. The supported is denoted by a horizontal line on a diagram that connects more than two upper parts.

A slight support or resistance will cause the trends to continue while reversing through strong support or resistance. The traders tend to buy support while others sell against the resistance turning its value into rewarding foresight.

Summary of the Support or Resistance Trading

1. Each morning, when you create your daily watch list, look immediately at the day cards on your watch list and find the support or resistance area.
2. Control the price action in these areas in a 5-minute chart. If an indecisive candle is formed in this area, this is the level confirmation, and you enter the operation. Generally, to minimize the risk, you should buy closely as possible. The stop is your pause and should be done no more than 5 minutes under the support or resistance levels.
3. Advances are to expect on the next support or resistance levels.
4. Don't close your trade not unless it already reached its profit aim or extends another support or resistance levels.
5. Selling positions are commonly happening close the profit aim or support or resistance levels. Then, you set your stop to reach the entry or breakeven point.

6. Closing your shares nearby to the middle position of cash level when there are no evident of support or resistance levels.

Develop Your Strategy

You must still find your place in the market. You may be a 1-minute or a 5-minute trader; you may be a 60-minute trader. Some may be daily or weekly traders (swing traders). There's a place in the market for everyone. Consider what you are learning in this book as pieces of a puzzle that together make up the bigger picture of trading. You're going to acquire some pieces here; you're going to pick up pieces on your own from your reading and research, and, overall, you will create a puzzle that will develop into your unique trading strategy. This book will help you develop a strategy that is going to work for you, your personality, your account size and your risk tolerance.

The key is that you master a strategy. Once you have a strategy in the market, you can become a trader without breaking your bank account. This is more than sitting on a chair. Remember that the more time spent looking at your chart, the further you will learn. It is a kind of job where you survive until you can do it. You can start throwing later, but first, you must master only one strategy. It can be the exchange of VWAP, it can be a bullish indicator momentum strategy, it can be a reversal strategy, or it can create its own strategy. Reduce the options, convert this area of strength into a viable strategy and use that strategy to survive until you can develop others.

It is absolutely crucial for each trader to act on a strategy. Plan an exchange and change the plan. You have to act a strategy. If you exchange real money, you must have a written strategy and historical data to verify that it is worth trading with real money. You cannot change your plan if you have already entered the operation and have an open position.

The truth about traders is that they fail. They lose money, and a large percentage of those traders are not getting the education that you are receiving from this book. They're going to be using live trading strategies that are not even hammered out, they will be haphazardly trading a little of this and a little of that until their account is gone, and then they will wonder what happened.

You don't want to live trade a new strategy until you've proven that it's worth investing in. You may practice three months on a simulator, and then trade small size with real money for one month, and then go back to the simulator to work on your mistakes or practice new strategies for another three months. There is no shame in going back to a simulator at any stage of your day trading career. Even experienced and professional traders, when they want to develop a new strategy, test it out on a live simulator first.

Your focus, while reading this book and practicing in simulated accounts, should be to develop a strategy worth trading, and it's my pleasure to assist you with that process. Remember, the market is always going to be there. You don't need to rush this. A day trading career is a marathon and not a sprint. It's not about making $50,000 by the end of next week. It's about developing a set of skills that will last a lifetime.

Chapter 5: Successful Trading Guide and Money Management

The philosophy in the business is that you only have to master a few solid configurations to be consistently profitable. In fact, a simple trading method, which consists of a few minimal configurations, confusion and stress helps reduce and allows you to focus more on the psychological aspect of the negotiation, which really distinguishes the winners from the losers.

Now that you have learned the basics of some business strategies let's take a closer look at the actual planning and negotiation process. Now understand the configuration you want to act, but as a beginner trader, you will have a difficult time in advance to plan a trade and start. It is very common to have a good set-up, but then go into a trade at the wrong time or let the money go and at the same time make money from others. I think the solution is to develop a process for your trade. Plan an exchange and change a plan.

Trading process:
- Routine morning activities
- Create an observation list
- Consolidate a negotiation plan
- Start the trade accordingly
- Implementation and execution of plans
- Diary and reflection

You must remember that what makes an operation profitable is the correct execution of all the steps in the previous process. Write your reasons for entering and leaving each operation. Everyone can read this book or dozens of other books, but few people have the discipline to function properly. You may have a good configuration, but choose an incorrect action to trade. An action manipulated by computers and institutional traders. You may find an appropriate action to negotiate but negotiate at the wrong time. A bad entry will ruin your plan, and eventually, you will lose your money. You can find a good stock for trade and enter a trade properly, but if you do not get the right one, it will become an unprofitable trade, a loss of decision. All the steps of the process are important.

Think about something important that you often do in your life and then think about how you can do better. Now think about how you are doing right now. This is a great mind process for traders. When making an exchange, you must make sure you focus on the right things, before you start and negotiate. Forming a system for this proper process will eliminate majority of the emotional dependencies that traders encounter when they try to get in and manage an operation.

Final Rule

Profitable trade should not encompass any emotional aspect. If you are a sensitive trader, you will lose your money.

Training and practice give you an overview of what is involved in the action, how you act and how you can grow and develop your skills. Once you have a perspective of what matters, you can continue to identify the specific processes on which you should focus. The key to success is the exact knowledge of their processes. You often learn them the hard way, losing money.

Sticking to your negotiation plan and the discipline inherent in your negotiation methodology has caused a snowball effect of positive habits in your life in general, and these habits have contributed to more commercial success. For example, start your negotiation actions by following the same routine when you wake up in the sunrise. You always do a race in the morning before the negotiation session begins. For example, you live in Vancouver, Canada, and the market opens at 6:30, your time. You wake up every morning at 5 o'clock. You go from 5 to 5:45 p. m. (Usually between 7 and 10 kilometers (or 4 to 6 miles). You come home, you shower and at 6 o'clock you begin to develop your plan.

If your body was not active before operating, you would make bad decisions. There are scientific studies that show that aerobic exercise has a positive effect on the decision-making process. People who regularly participate in aerobic exercise (e.g., at least 30 minutes) have higher values for neuropsychological functions and performance tests of cognitive functions, such as attention control, inhibition control, flexibility cognitive, working memory update and the speed of processing capacity and the measurement of information.

In day trading, it is not enough to be better than the average. You have to surpass the crowd to win in the daily trade. Regrettably, most of the people who were attracted to day trading are the impulsive, plungers, and selfish ones – those who think that the world should provide them more than what they have.

This reality does not mean to say you have to be like or act like them. Note that in order to win, you need to develop self-discipline. Your mindset and behavior are far different from the losers. Analyze yourself, disregard the deceptions, and change your old negative ways. I understand that in a way it is difficult, however, if you want to succeed in day trading, you need to work hard for it. You need not only to learn how day trading works but to improve your behavior and personality too. A successful trader is smart, motivated, and focused.

Now let's go back to the negotiation: as already mentioned, trade cannot be considered a hobby. You have to take the trade seriously. So you get up at 5 in the morning, you walk for 30 to 45 minutes, you shower, you dress, and you eat porridge for breakfast before you start your trading session at 6 in the morning. You are awake, alert and motivated when you sit down and start building your watch list. This morning, the routine of your mental preparation has tremendously helped you get to the market. So, whatever you do, the morning starts in a similar way to paying invaluable dividends. Waking up and washing your face with water 15 minutes in advance will give you little time to prepare for the opening of the market. Sitting on the computer in pajamas or underwear does not make you attack the market.

Your follow-up list comes from a standard analysis that you use every morning. You will be less likely to get mixed up to other stuff because you are sure that the stock of this scanner has the best chance of operating. Review each action, in the same way, using a checklist to see if it really is marketable to you. Your watch list will be created at 6:15 a.m. and will not add anything after that time since there will not be enough time to review new stocks and plan an operation. So you can see the tickers on our watch list 15 minutes before the opening. This really takes you to another step in your process.

In the 15 minutes prior to opening, you will see the tickers on your watch list and develop trading plans for them based on the price action you see. This is the most difficult part and requires experience, knowledge, and education. Many traders fail in this step.

When the bell rings at 6:30 a.m., your plans are recorded in the notebooks because it can be so easily missed out each of the open tickers you saw.

What is your next move if it is set on the long one? How about your next move if it turns out the opposite? What are your assumptions on the actions you made? How feasible are profit aims? What part should you establish your stop? Does your profit frame good enough to negotiate? If you ask these questions when planning your exchange, you have a clear advantage, because then you can continue and follow a battle plan. If it's close to your face, you can easily emphasize it, and that will eliminate the fear you felt when the bell rang. All you do in the opening is find your signal and activate the exchange.

Upon checking your watch list, you saw that Sarepta Therapeutics Inc (NASDAQ: SRPT) had a 15% difference. They knew that interest in buying shares was low. Who would dare to buy if shares fell overnight by 15%? In fact, most investors are trying to go out and sell before it goes down as if there is something really bad about the company. They could not find support or resistance in the vicinity, so opt for VWAP and choose a short VWAP operation.

Once the stock is configured, an entry is signaled and activated; you will enter without questioning (well, that is the plan). Sometimes you can appreciate yourself, but not too often. You have set my profit objectives in your trading plan, as well as the technical level at which you will be going to your stops, so after entering, concentrate only on my brands and your reservation benefit.

There are some who say that the hardest part of negotiating is knowing when to leave. It can be very difficult to stop trading too soon if you do not have an established plan. If you have a plan in advance and you meet it, you are more likely to make your payroll work and reduce your losses quickly, rather than the opposite. This is also useful to keep your emotions in check during the trade.

Once the exchange is over, you will think about how well your plan worked and how well you have done what you wrote. Most of your exchanges will be considered at night when you review and recap your operations from that day. You should ask yourself: "Which part did I do well?", "Are there any mistakes I have done?" And "Should I have sold myself before?" These are utterly crucial questions for the buildup of your trade.

Be noted that there is fact that even if you have obtained good profits, that still does not mean that you are an excellent trader.

Being a good trader is able to determine the importance of both sides of the table.

First write or take a video summary of the trade and everything that comes to mind at your school, then combine it with other previous lessons and use them all as a reference for the future. Some lessons are more difficult compared to others, but rest assured that it will only improve over time. You just need some time to absorb all the knowledge and details, and then implement them.

Why is this trade process important? This process is important because it describes how things are prepared for an operation and then keep the focus for execution. It helps filter social, emotional noise and gives you a better sight for a more rewarding victory.

As long you keep focus and implement on the right processes, you may be on the right path to trading success.

Conclusion

In this book, we have discussed different trading tactics. Some of the day trading tactics are more widely used than others and has each own positives and negatives. Moreover, it is up to the individual trader which day trading tactic he is going to use. This is the reason why a day trader must carefully learn the basics and strategies in day trading to know what suits there trading style.

Other than knowing your strategy, traits are also needed to develop in order to rise to successful trading. These include being responsible, committed, patient, focused, adaptable, independent, and mentally disciplined.

- Responsibility: Know that you are accountable for all the investments and trading decisions you made. In case of losing, you should still act rationally by determining your mistakes and making sure to prevent it next time.
- Commitment: Successful traders are dedicating time and putting a lot of effort to improve their

abilities. They make sure they understand well how the companies, markets, trading tactics, and their own strategies affect their investment. Day traders are consistently looking for ways to be smarter in their negotiation.

- Patient: Day trading requires waiting. You need to know when the timing is right. Hence, it requires practice. There are times when you might enter or exit on the unwanted times which will help you in the future to be careful when to wait for better entry and exit. Be patient until you need to take action without thinking twice. Never put your patience off.

- Adaptable: If you have fully understood all the day trading tactics in this book under different market conditions, you can now use them accordingly. A day trader must observe the price level on a daily basis and utilize the tactics effectively.

- Independent: You bought this book to serve as your guide to trading. You might also look for some trading videos on the internet or look for seminars related to day trading. However, no matter who helps or guides you, it is you who will determine your day trading success.

This means that you don't have to rely on others. You should be able to develop your instinct on choosing the path that is most profitable. Once you found out which day trading tactic works for you, opinions of other people won't be necessary anymore.

- Mentally disciplined: The success of day trading depends on the trader's mental state. This covers the trader's ability to decide and be confident in his strategies. Moreover, most of the successful day traders also set rules and guides and follow them. They make sure to follow them no matter how difficult it may be. Any delay from the things they follow might lead to a day trading breakdown.

- All the day trading tactics or methods stated in the book carry a risk. But, if you are mentally disciplined enough, you won't allow the potential for success not to achieve.

The success of the day trading is based on three essential skills.

1. Determining the power balance between buyers and sellers and placing them on a profitable group.
2. Practicing money and trading management.
3. Acquiring self-discipline to follow your trading plan to prevent losing you in the negotiations and making emotive decisions.

After reading this book, you should be able to make a better decision about whether the trading day is right for you or not. The day trading has a requirement that one should have a practical way of thinking, developed self-discipline and possessed a set of skills that others don't have. Interestingly, most traders are also poker players. You enjoy the speculation and the stimulation that results from it. Although poker is a way of betting, daily business is not.

Day trading is not a game – it is scientific, a skillful work, and a serious business. It is not simply buying and selling shares, though it can be done in seconds. A day trader knows how to make decisions intelligently and quickly without involving emotive aspects. If not, your money is lost.

After you have decided and decided that you want to start the day of trading:

- You must receive adequate training. You should never start your daily commercial career with real money.
- You must develop your strategy once you have your simulated account.
- You must practice with the sums of money that you exchange in real life.
- You must contribute to your education and reflect your business strategy.

- You must join a dealership community. Trading alone is very difficult and can be emotionally overwhelming.
- Gradually, your judgment will be developed. Your instinct helps you to decide when to trade or not. Remember that a successful trader is an independent thinker.

Best wishes, Darrell Frost

www.ingramcontent.com/pod-product-compliance
Lightning Source LLC
Chambersburg PA
CBHW070125230526
45472CB00004B/1427